Grandma Chickenlegs

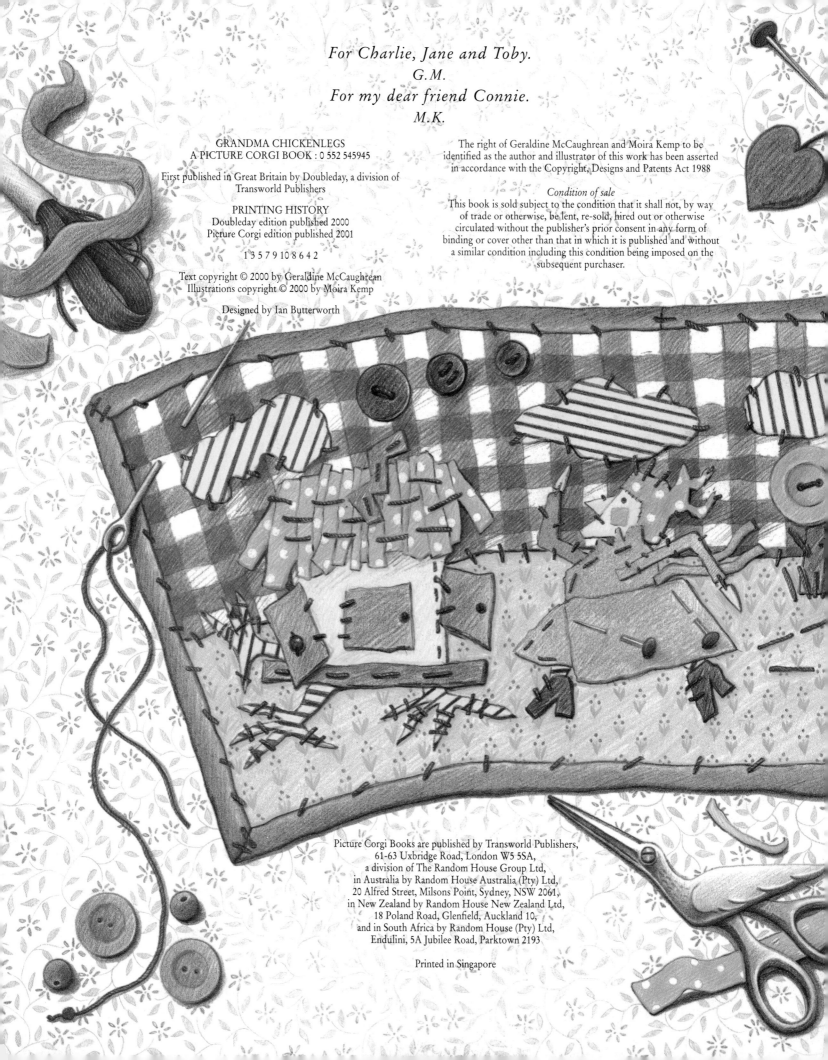

For Charlie, Jane and Toby.
G.M.
For my dear friend Connie.
M.K.

GRANDMA CHICKENLEGS
A PICTURE CORGI BOOK : 0 552 545945

First published in Great Britain by Doubleday, a division of
Transworld Publishers

PRINTING HISTORY
Doubleday edition published 2000
Picture Corgi edition published 2001

1 3 5 7 9 10 8 6 4 2

Designed by Ian Butterworth

Picture Corgi Books are published by Transworld Publishers,
61-63 Uxbridge Road, London W5 5SA,
a division of The Random House Group Ltd,
in Australia by Random House Australia (Pty) Ltd,
20 Alfred Street, Milsons Point, Sydney, NSW 2061,
in New Zealand by Random House New Zealand Ltd,
18 Poland Road, Glenfield, Auckland 10,
and in South Africa by Random House (Pty) Ltd,
Endulini, 5A Jubilee Road, Parktown 2193

Printed in Singapore

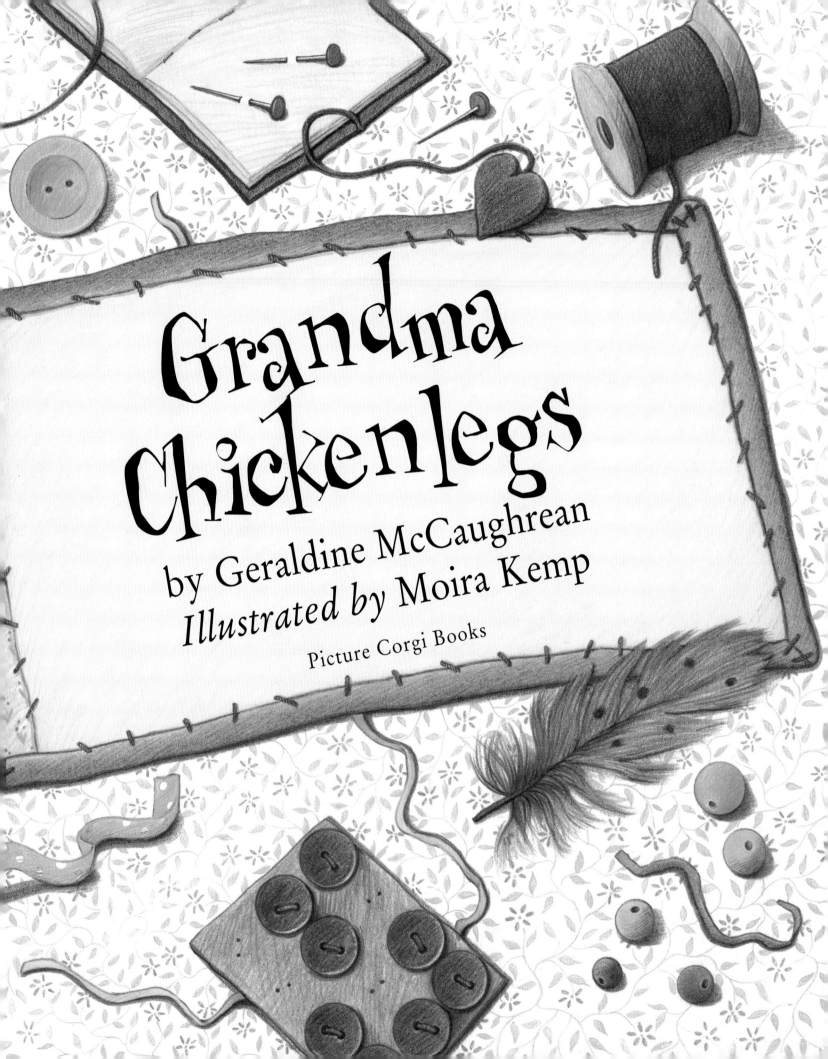

Grandma Chickenlegs

by Geraldine McCaughrean
Illustrated by Moira Kemp

Picture Corgi Books

One day, when a sudden fall of snow rubbed out the flowers, Tatia's mother died. In saying goodbye, she gave Tatia only a kiss, a rag doll and a word of warning:

"Be giving and forgiving, dearest dear ... and beware of Grandma Chickenlegs!"

Tatia's father loved his little daughter better than milk or meat or money.

But he was a merchant and had to travel abroad for months at a time. So, thinking Tatia needed a mother, he married again - a woman with eyes as sharp as needles and a soul as thin as a thread.

The woman already had two daughters of her own and had no mind to mind a third. But she pretended to love Tatia, for the sake of her father's fortune. Besides, little girls can easily be got rid of when no-one is looking.

No sooner did Tatia's father leave on business than her life changed to winter. Stepmother told her, "You must clean the house, cook the supper and milk the cow; mend the roof, wash the clothes, feed the pigs and set the fire."

Sweet natured as she was, Tatia did not complain (well, only a little perhaps, to her dear doll, Drooga). "Ah well," she sighed. "Soon Daddy will be home again."

Stepmother gave her very little food, but of course Tatia had the scrapings from the pots to eat. Anyway, young girls cannot help growing. One day her smock was just too small to wear any more.

"Tatia, my dear child!" cried Stepmother. "Your smock is too small. I must sew you a new one. Fetch me my sewing box!"

Tatia was astonished. So were her stepsisters. "Make us smocks first, Mama!" they whined.

Stepmother ignored them and opened her sewing box. "Well, well. Look at that. Oh dear. Such a shame. No needle. Now Tatia will have to go to Grandma Chickenlegs and borrow one."

Tatia gasped and ran to her room. Pulling her rag doll from her pocket she hugged her close and said, "Oh what shall I do, Drooga dear? I'm sure Grandma Chickenlegs will be the death of me!"

Her dolly blinked its silk-sewn eyes and opened its wool-sewn lips. "Tie your hair with a ribbon, take a clean handkerchief, and remember what your mother said. Then all will be well."

So Tatia did as Drooga said, and set off through the forest. As Stepmother watched her go, she spat on the step and said to her daughters, "That's the last we shall see of her!"

On and on Tatia walked through the fields and woods until she came to a dark forest and there, in the shadow of a gnarled elm tree, stood a crooked house. At last Tatia understood how their neighbour had got her strange name. It was not the old lady who had chicken legs. It was her house!

Around the garden, on four scratching, paltry poultry legs ran the bleak shack. Its fence was made from whitening bones, the gateposts topped with skulls. The front door swung on its hinges squealing like a thing in pain. Its keyhole gnashed tiny, tinny teeth. Beside the house stood a giant grinding bowl and in it a huge stone pestle.

Before Tatia could even knock, the door flew open, and there stood Grandma Chickenlegs looking so fierce that her own house trembled and knocked at its chickeny knees.

"What do you want with the Baba Yaga?!" she screamed. "What do you want with Grandma Chickenlegs?"

"Please, Grandma," whispered Tatia, curtseying. "A needle, to sew myself a smock."

"You shall have it if you earn it!" grinned the witch, baring iron teeth as sharp and snapping as a mantrap. "But first come in and eat."

Indoors, the shack looked more comfortable. There was a polished table and a four-poster feather bed, a weaver's loom and a big open fire. The witch brought Tatia white bread rolls and golden butter, sizzling bacon and rich red wine. She showed her a silver needle, too.

"Weave at my loom for one night, and this is yours," said the witch.

"Thank you, Grandma."

In the flickering light of a hundred candles, other eyes were watching - a small black cat and a snarling dog.

"Hello," said Tatia and smiled, but the cat only spat. The front door went on squealing.

Tatia began to eat. But the animals both looked so famished that when Grandma Chickenlegs went out of the room, Tatia gave the bacon to the cat and the rolls to the dog. She smeared the butter on the door hinges, too, to stop them squeaking. From the kitchen, the Baba Yaga called her animals, and whispered to them.

"I wonder what she is saying, Drooga," said Tatia to her dolly. The dolly blinked her silk-sewn eyes and opened her wool-sewn lips. "She says, 'Heat the water and fill the bath. You know I like my food washed before I eat it.'"

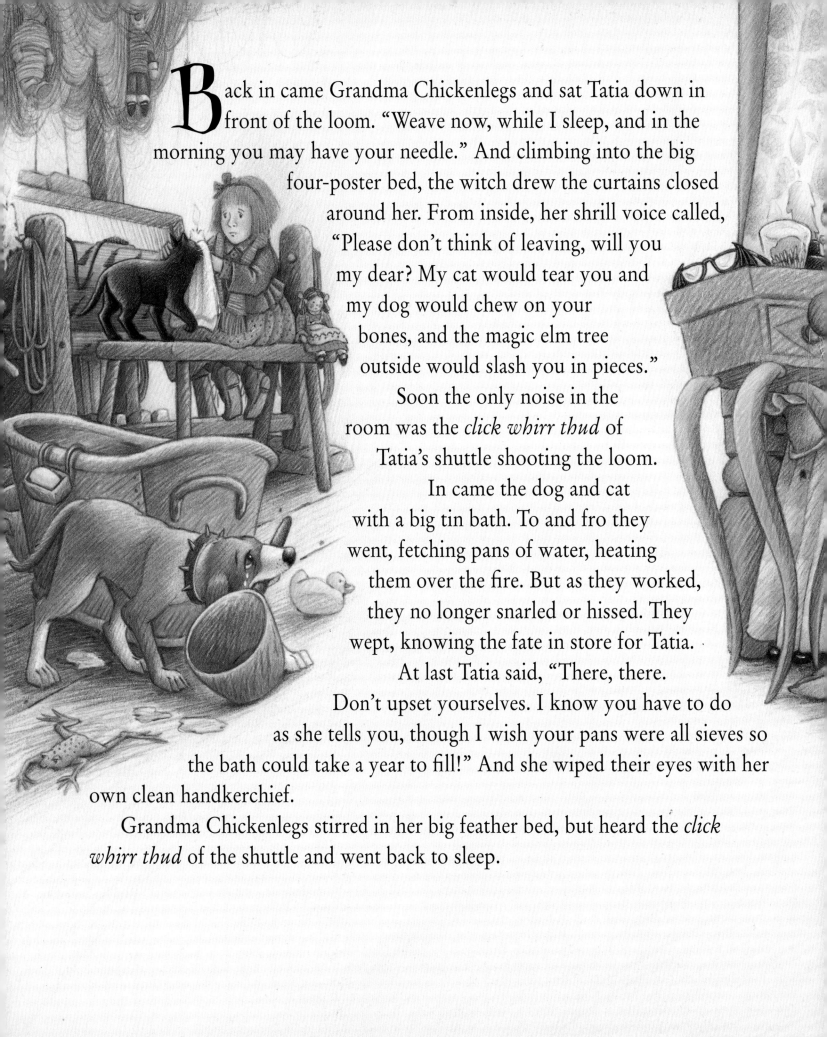

ack in came Grandma Chickenlegs and sat Tatia down in front of the loom. "Weave now, while I sleep, and in the morning you may have your needle." And climbing into the big four-poster bed, the witch drew the curtains closed around her. From inside, her shrill voice called, "Please don't think of leaving, will you my dear? My cat would tear you and my dog would chew on your bones, and the magic elm tree outside would slash you in pieces." Soon the only noise in the room was the *click whirr thud* of Tatia's shuttle shooting the loom. In came the dog and cat with a big tin bath. To and fro they went, fetching pans of water, heating them over the fire. But as they worked, they no longer snarled or hissed. They wept, knowing the fate in store for Tatia. At last Tatia said, "There, there. Don't upset yourselves. I know you have to do as she tells you, though I wish your pans were all sieves so the bath could take a year to fill!" And she wiped their eyes with her own clean handkerchief.

Grandma Chickenlegs stirred in her big feather bed, but heard the *click whirr thud* of the shuttle and went back to sleep.

All of a sudden, Dog trotted over, a red towel in its mouth. "Take this towel and run. If the Baba Yaga comes after you, throw it down on the ground."

Then Cat was there, too, a comb embedded in its black fur. "Take this comb and run, and if the Baba Yaga is still after you, throw it down on the ground."

Drooga whispered in Tatia's ear, "They're right. Go. Run. I'll keep weaving until you are safely away."

But Tatia shook her head. "Oh, I couldn't go anywhere without you, Drooga! I'd be too afraid! If I go, you must come with me."

"In that case," said Cat, "I shall do the weaving."

So out of the door went Tatia, her dolly in her pocket. The hinges would have creaked and woken the witch, but Tatia had smeared them with butter, hadn't she? And though the Baba Yaga stirred in her sleep, she heard the *click whirr thud* of the shuttle and dozed off again.

Outside, Tatia almost screamed out loud. There, against the moon, like the skeleton of a dragon, loomed the magic elm tree, its twiggy talons spread to snatch and catch.

Tatia pushed her hand into her pocket, pulled out her rag doll and held the woollen lips to her ear. Then she knew what to do. She untied her hair and shook it loose. Standing on tiptoe, she tied the ribbon to a twig of the magic elm.

Away went her ribbon, away went the branch, as the elm stood aside and let them pass. But its twigs accidentally scratched against the cottage wall, and the Baba Yaga stirred in her sleep.

Click whirr thud went the cat's shuttle (though it had never tried its paw at weaving before), and the Baba Yaga went back to sleep.

Not for long. Suddenly the loom fell over with a clatter. Grandma Chickenlegs woke, hungry. She dragged open the bed curtains and saw...

... Cat cradled in a hopeless tangle of broken threads, and Dog hiding in the tin bath. Of little Tatia there was no trace.

"Villains! Traitors! Fools!" shrieked the witch. Grandma Chickenlegs danced with rage.

"Why did you not tear her and chew her and slash her and STOP her!?"

"In all the years I've served you," said the cat, "you've never given me so much as a rind. She gave me bacon."

"In all the years I've served you," said the dog, "you've never given me so much as a crust. She gave me white rolls."

"In all the years I've served you," said the door, "you've never given me so much as a drop of oil. She smeared me with best butter."

"In all the years I've served you," said the elm tree, "you've never so much as hung your washing on me to dry. She tied a ribbon in my hair. See? Pretty, isn't it?"

She leapt into the giant grinding bowl and, grabbing the huge pestle, began to punt her magic vessel through the air. Faster than a chariot she flew, while her chicken-legged house ran after her.

"You won't get away from me!" she screamed, as in the distance, Tatia came into sight.

However fast Tatia and Drooga ran, they could no more outrun the Baba Yaga than take wing. When Tatia looked round, she saw the iron teeth gaping, the eyes ablaze...

"Throw down the towel that Dog gave you!" cried Drooga. At once, the towel stretched itself along the ground, a wide rushing river full of sharp rocks, with steep banks and white-water rapids.

Its magic was too strong for birds or witches to fly over it, and the Baba Yaga had to land her grinding bowl and climb out.

Down on her knees she got and began to drink. Slurp went the water through those iron teeth, gurgle went the river down the Baba Yaga's throat.

"Rivers won't save you!" she screamed as she leapt back aboard her magic bowl.

Soon she had Tatia again in sight, and almost within her grasp...

"Throw down the comb that Cat gave you!" cried Drooga. And up sprang pine trees - hundreds and thousands of dense, dark pine trees, their trunks so close together that not a stoat nor a weasel could have squeezed between them.

Flying too fast to stop, the magic grinding bowl crashed into the trees and the Baba Yaga fell out on her head.

Like a headless chicken she danced with uncontrollable temper. Her voice screeched over the treetops:

"Forests won't save you!"

And baring her iron teeth, she began to champ and chew on the tree trunks, spitting out twigs and splinters.

But her teeth were wet from drinking the river. Long before the forest was eaten, the iron between her jaws began to rust, and Grandma Chickenlegs had to give up her chase.

When her cottage came trotting along, she went inside it and slammed the door, and the bleak shack ran off, on its four chicken legs, to another country, another story, another secret corner of the tell-tale world.

Tatia was still running, though, running without looking back, or even where she was going. She ran - oof! - right into a merchant leading his horse along the road.

"Tatia?"

"Daddy!" cried Tatia, and hugged her father, and told him everything, just as

it had happened. When they got home, Tatia's father called his new wife and her two daughters and took out a pair of scissors.

He cut their fine silk dresses from neck to hem, and their six cotton petticoats, too. Then he turned them out of the house in nothing but their drawers, and told them never to come back.

"But we must have clothes!" they wailed.

"Then you had best go and borrow a needle from Grandma Chickenlegs," said Tatia and firmly shut the door.

Fortunately, her father had brought home plenty of cloth for smocks - enough for new ones in red and yellow and blue. Not just for clothes, either, but for a cushion and a rug. Which is just as well, because next day Dog and Cat arrived - Drooga had told them the way.

All five of them lived together in perfect happiness after that, without a care in the world.

... or so Drooga told me, yesterday.